You Are So Precious

I Wouldn't Trade You
For Anything In The World

A Children's Story of
Love and Geography

Written by Kimberly L Novak
Illustrated by Syifa Hanna

You are so precious;
I wouldn't trade you for anything in the world.

Georgia, USA

Ebook ISBN-13: 979-8-9897168-0-7
Paperback ISBN-13: 979-8-9897168-1-4

Dedication

In honor of Violet Novak
for her loving words.

Dedicated to my daughter,
my greatest treasure. KLN

To all the wonderful readers,
it was you who motivated me to
illustrate the beautiful words in this
book. SH

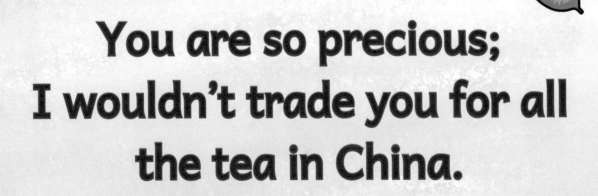

You are so precious;
I wouldn't trade you for all
the tea in China.

You are so precious;
I wouldn't trade you for all the
shiny gold in South Africa.

You are so precious;
I wouldn't trade you for all
the beautiful tulips
in the Netherlands.

You are so precious;
I wouldn't trade you for all the
delicious blueberries in the
United States of America.

You are so precious;
I wouldn't trade you for all the
freezing ice in Antarctica.

You are so precious;
I wouldn't trade you for all the
colorful fish swimming
in the Pacific Ocean.

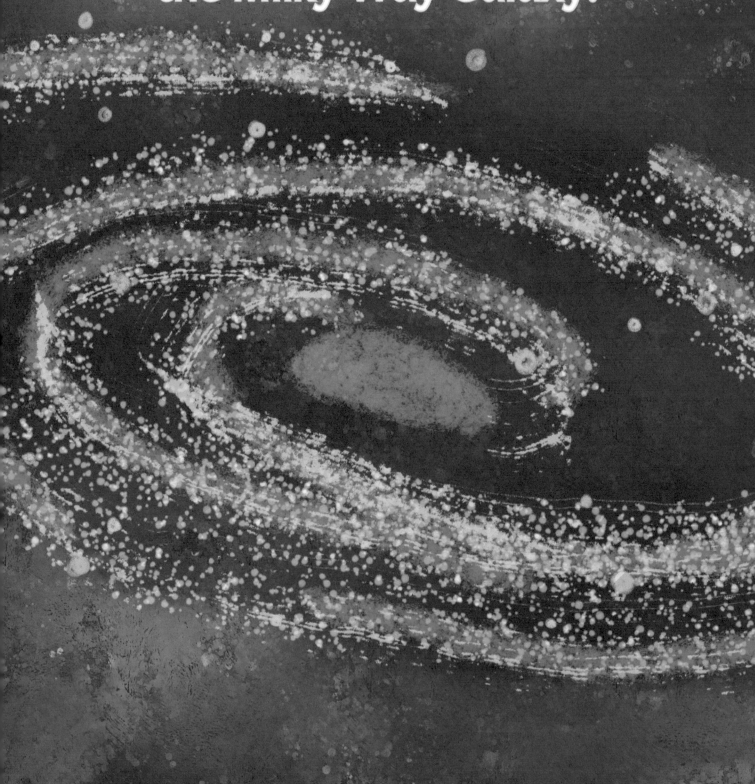

You are so precious;
I wouldn't trade you for all the
twinkling stars in
the Milky Way Galaxy.

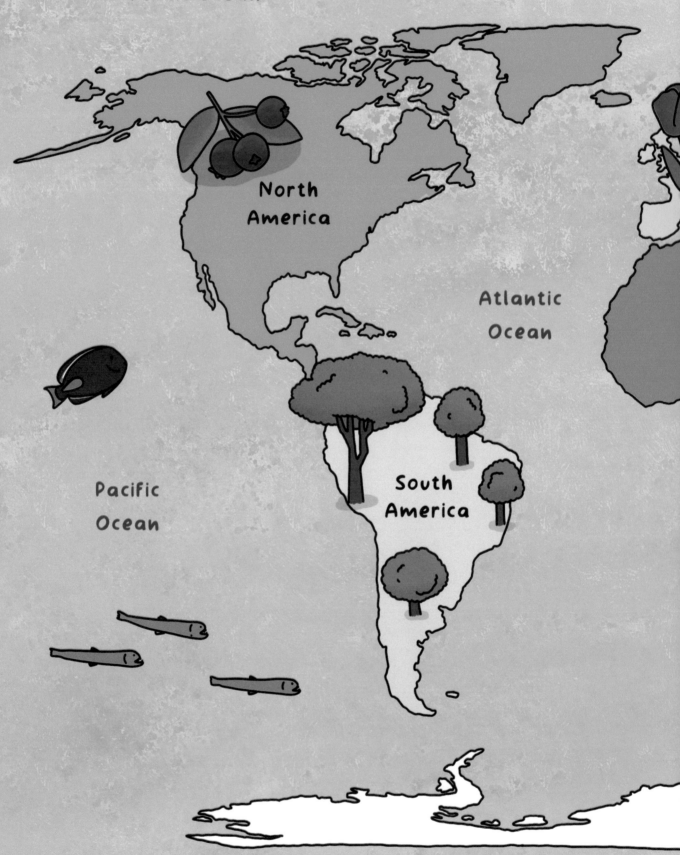

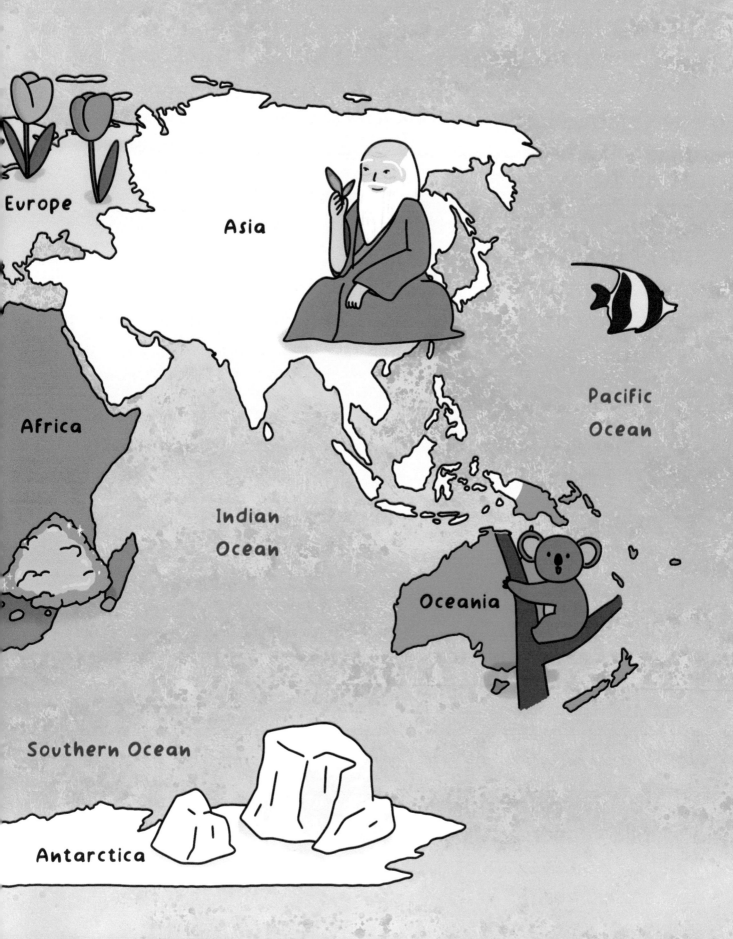

Europe

Asia

Africa

Pacific
Ocean

Indian
Ocean

Oceania

Southern Ocean

Antarctica

Fun Facts About the Places in This Book

Do you drink your tea with sugar, milk or lemon?

CHINA produces over 30% of all tea worldwide, including green and black teas. Tea is made from the leaves of a tree (*Camellia*). Emperor Shennong introduced tea to China in 2737 BCE.

Do you like the color gold?

More than 40% of the world's mined gold comes from **SOUTH AFRICA.** The first gold rush (1886) in the Witwatersrand Basin created Johannesburg. Gold is used in jewelry, computers, televisions, and medical devices.

Do you have a favorite animal?

Koalas (*Phascolarctos*) are a type of arboreal marsupial that eat eucalyptus leaves. Endemic to **AUSTRALIA**, koalas are now on the endangered list.

What is your favorite flower?

In the 17th century, the Dutch Golden Age saw the rise of tulip (*Tulipa*) mania. Today, the **NETHERLANDS** grows over 8 billion blooms a year.

How many blueberries can you fit in your mouth?

The **UNITED STATES OF AMERICA** grows and collects over 200 million pounds of blueberries (*Vaccinium*) each year. Blueberries have lots of nutrition and are found in many dessert recipes.

Have you climbed a tree?

The Amazon Rainforest, located in **BRAZIL**, is the biggest rainforest in the world. Within it is the world's largest river called the Amazon. The rainforest has the greatest biodiversity of life on Earth, including the 250-foot-tall Angelim Vermhelo (*Dinizia*) tree.

Can you imagine penguins eating ice cream?

ANTARCTICA has five million square miles of ice, which is bigger than the USA and Mexico combined. On average, it is over a mile thick. There are seven species of penguins (*Spheniscidae*) that have made several adaptations to call this icy continent home.

Do you have a pet fish?

The **PACIFIC OCEAN** is the largest and deepest of the five oceanic divisions. The Bristlemouth (*Gonostomatidae*) is the most common fish in the world. It likes to swim deep, and some of them produce a bioluminescent light (kind of like a night light).

What is your favorite constellation of stars?

Our solar system lies along an arm of the spiral **MILKY WAY GALAXY**. There are 100 billion stars in our galaxy. Each star is a ball of energy, and some have planets orbiting around them. We like to group stars into constellations with names like Orion or Aquarius.

Learning and Activity Pages for Kids

(If you want to preserve the book, feel free to copy these two pages)

A **Natural Resource** is something that comes from nature (sun, air, land, water, or living things) and is used by people to stay alive or make their world better.

Manufacturing is the process of converting the **raw materials** of a natural resource into a usable **product**.

Research it!
Ask your family and friends, or do some research. What are some natural resources from where you live?

Match it!
Can you match the resource to the country which produces the most?

Alpacas	Canada
Avocados	Costa Rica
Bananas	Côte d'Ivoire
Cocoa (Chocolate)	India
Coconuts	Indonesia
Ice Cream	Mexico
Pineapples	New Zealand
Polar Bears	Peru

Game it!
Try the animal, plant, or mineral game. Think of a natural resource, but keep it a surprise (don't share). Let your family or friends ask you questions that you can only answer "yes" or "no" to, such as "Is it a plant?", "Do we eat it?", "Is it purple?". See how many questions it takes for them to discover the surprise answer!

Color it!

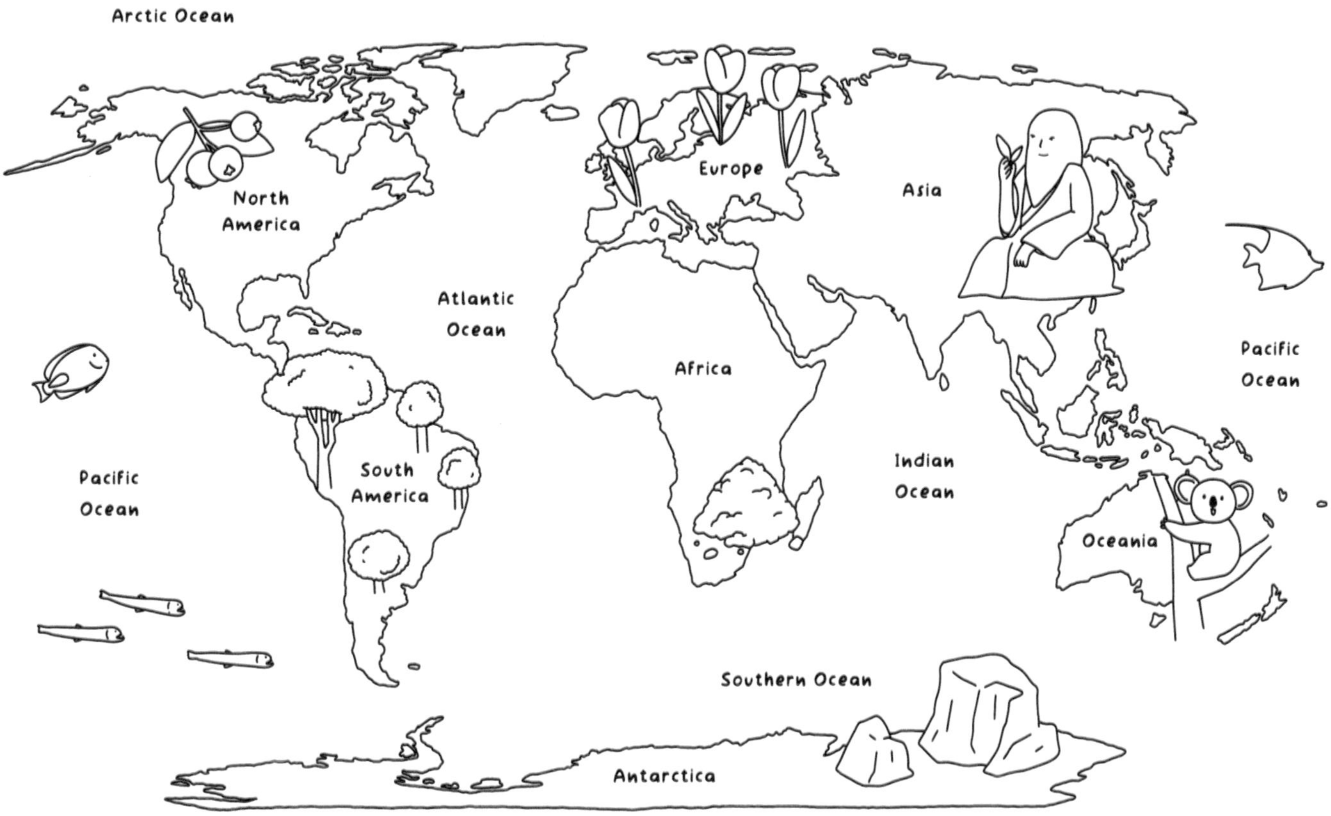

Answers: Alpacas - Peru / Avocados - Mexico / Bananas - India / Cocoa - Cote d'Ivoire / Coconuts - Indonesia / Ice Cream - New Zealand / Pineapples - Costa Rica / Polar Bears - Canada

Information for Parents, Teachers, and Caretakers

All children need a sense of belonging and of place. My grandmother understood this when she first told me in words of exchange how valuable I was to her. As you read and discuss this picture book, you can help the young people in your life make connections to their personal environment and resources.

Children enjoy kinesthetic activities such as swimming like a fish, waddling like a penguin, climbing a tree like a koala, and picking imaginary blueberries to eat. Let them show you their favorite movement.

The children in this book discover the different countries and continents of the world. This concept connects to elementary geography standards, including relationships that shape our cultures and globe.

Elementary STEM, Science, and CTE courses all include a topic on natural resources. In order to meet the future needs of people, we must understand what resources we have now. You can find many family and educator resources through USDA and US DOI.

You can use the background information for each resource and location to explore place value by counting the number of zeros or percent with a simple colored circle to practice math skills.

Our physical world is huge, like stars, and tiny, like bits of gold dust. Children can use various art tools and techniques, such as clay to make a planet, and repurposed materials to represent natural resources to connect their art to their world.

The concepts in this book can be used to support three of the key areas of Social Emotional Learning (SEL), including self-awareness, relationships, and social awareness. You can discover more about standards-based learning for well-being through organizations such as CASEL.

Author

Kimberly Novak draws inspiration from her experiences as a traveler, teacher, and parent to share the wonders of ourselves and our world over a cup of tea or video chat. This is her debut book based on a loving message from her grandmother. She currently lives with her daughter and cat in Georgia, USA.

Artist

Syifa Hanna is a self-taught artist. Before becoming a children's book illustrator, she designed fan art, doodles, and icons in a cute style. Her first children's project is a series of five books. She currently lives and works in East Java, Indonesia.

Thank you for reading!

You Are So Precious; I Wouldn't Trade You For Anything In The World.

Feedback is appreciated and makes a positive difference.

We hope you will stay in touch!

We welcome your stories and pictures of you enjoying your treasures.

You can also access additional learning and activity resources.

Email us at authorkimberlylnovak@gmail.com

www.facebook.com/authorkimberlylnovak
www.amazon.com/author/kimberlylnovak

Made in the USA
Columbia, SC
23 June 2024

37397759R00018